31 Daily Inspirations for Caregivers

One Day, One Breath, One Step at a Time

Judy Micale

First Printing, 2013
Printed in the United States of America

Cover Design and photograph by Judy Micale

Liability Disclaimer

This book is designed to provide information and motivation to the readers. It is sold with the understanding that the author is not engaged to render any type of psychological, legal, or any other kind of professional advice. The content is the sole expression and opinion of its author. No warranties or guarantees are expressed or implied by the author's choice to include any of the content in this volume. The author shall not be liable for any physical, psychological, emotional, financial, or commercial damages, including, but not limited to, special, incidental, consequential or other damages. You are responsible for your own choices, actions, and results.

ACKNOWLEDGEMENTS

I am so grateful for my family and friends all year round and just want to thank everyone who has supported me. I am so blessed to have friends who have encouraged me throughout this experience and have given me not only verbal support and encouragement but have sent positive thoughts and prayers my way. You know who you are and I thank each and every one of you. I want to send out a special thank you to my mom, without her this book would not have come to be. It is because of her love and support and our very special time together over the last several years that I am motivated to write daily inspirations. There were days I wrote them for myself and other days I wrote them for her. Each quote that you read in this book came from my love and experiences with caring for her. I hold that this book is read with the highest of intentions.

I also want to thank the women who were in the Writing a Kindle Book in a Weekend retreat that Candi Parker (of ParkerHouseBooks.com) held in August 2013. The energy and encouragement from all is unforgettable. I want to thank Candi for the encouragement and support she has provided. You are an awesome book coach! Thank you for helping to make my dream come true.

I also want to thank my editor Barbara Ann Cox who took the time to preview and tweak my creative thought. I appreciate your time and expertise.

PREFACE

I wrote this book to assist others in their journey of caring for a loved one. This book is for anyone who is a caregiver, whether they are a child caring for a parent, a parent taking care of a child or a professional caring for a patient/client. I hope that the quotes you find inside this book provide you with inspiration in continuing in your journey.

As I sit here and write this introduction the hummingbirds are flitting by and taking turns at the hummingbird feeder. They even argue at times, telling the others that it is their turn! I think this is a great symbolism for how we are as caretakers; we take turns being cared for and in turn caring for another.

This book is set up where the reader can read a quote and take time to meditate on that quote. I suggest you take a quote a day and reflect on it. The journal pages, which are included after each daily inspiration are blank so the reader can choose to write, draw or paste a picture to assist you in keeping track of your journey over the next 31 days.

I am in the process of working on the second book with more daily inspirations. Please keep in mind that this book is just to assist in encouraging and inspiring you, the reader; it is not meant as a therapeutic tool. If you are in any way overwhelmed and feel you may need to speak to someone, I encourage you to contact a specialist. Even caregivers need to reach out and ask for help. The greatest advice given to me was by another caretaker. She told me to rip the "S" off my chest and reach out for assistance. "What does the "S" stand for?" you may ask; why it stands for superwoman! Since I don't know anyone who possesses superpowers, I encourage you to do the same and rip that "S" off and ask for help.

I have a Facebook page for the book series please take a moment and "like" the page "Daily Inspirations for Caregivers". My vision for this page is that the caregiving community will have a site where they go and offer tips and tricks to assist others.

Judy Micale

September 2013

Table of Contents

DAY ONE – BREATHE, SMILE

One breath and one smile at a time is the mantra for today!

As caregivers, we need to remember to take each day as it comes. We are open and flexible to changes as they come. When we feel overwhelmed, we remember to breathe. The final piece, remembering that our smiles are empowering to those we care for as much as their smiles bring us joy.

DAY ONE JOURNAL ENTRY:

Take time today to consciously open yourself to the act of caring for another person. Remember in this process to ask yourself, "What is it that I am giving to this person?" and, "By giving what am I receiving?" Remember that in order to give you must be open to receiving; the process is a two way street. At the end of the day take time to journal what was given and received.

DAY ONE JOURNAL ENTRY:

Coincidentally I've opened this book on a Thursday. Thursday is a day I weekly pretty much devote to my mom's needs. I make all her appts. on Thurs. and take her to the pool on Thurs. Today no pool because she overdid last Saturday/last week the pool when the Drill Sergeant was leading the class. We got her a steroid shot in her knee which is bone on bone arthritic. She felt good for a day but then kicked too hard at water aerobics and is back in pain again. Her heel is the worst — she has a stone sized callous on her heel that digs into the bottom of her foot. Podiatrist Appt. in 2 wks!

DAY ONE JOURNAL ENTRY:

I've only recently come to the conclusion that I can balance my work/wife/caregiver time by having a weekly schedule, which I do anyway. MTW office worker/wife - Thurs/First part of Friday — daughter-caregiver — Fri evening wife — Sat. morning shopper/provider/bill payer/ME time Saturday evening wife, Sunday CATCH UP office worker, all overflow!! So even though that's the way I've been doing it, I hadn't codified it so when I was with Bart on say a wednesday night, I felt like I should be spending time w/ mom. But I shouldn't because it's not her time. No one can have all my time all the time. Not even me.

3

DAY ONE JOURNAL ENTRY:

I know that in giving I receive. It's important to slow down enough to realize it. I think devoting myself totally to whatever I'm doing at the moment is the only way to really receive. "Scheduling" will help with that, although I know there is no perfect system.

DAY TWO – IT IS WHAT IT IS

Today I am grateful for the fact that what is to be will be......don't second guess. Just go with it and let what transpires happen at its own pace.
We as human beings are prone to wanting to plan and fix things the way we "think" they should be. Today just let the day happen. Yes, it is okay to have a general plan but don't become so bogged down in what you plan that you can't enjoy the moment.

DAY TWO JOURNAL ENTRY:

This Journal entry is to be done at the end of the day. Reflect back over the day. Journal about what your original plans where and what changed. Remember to include the "hiccups" that occurred and see the positive pieces that came out of the unplanned parts of the day.

DAY TWO JOURNAL ENTRY:

DAY TWO JOURNAL ENTRY:

DAY TWO JOURNAL ENTRY:

DAY THREE – LAUGHTER & LOVE

Oh laughter and love -- what a great combination!

As caregivers, we do what we do out of love. It is so important to remember that we are not stuck caring for anyone. We have chosen to be a part of their life. We have chosen the path of a caregiver. If you no longer feel this way, then please take a moment today and remember the good parts of what you do. It is normal to become frustrated. However, if we take a moment to remember the good parts and the laughter, then we can keep on the path.

DAY THREE JOURNAL ENTRY:

As you begin your day today, remember the joy and good times you have had as a caregiver. What has caused you to stay? What makes you giggle? Take time today to share with those you care for the day's highlights. Ask them to share with you what their highlights were. At the end of the day record not only your responses but theirs as well. That way you have these wonderful memories in the future.

DAY THREE JOURNAL ENTRY:

DAY THREE JOURNAL ENTRY:

DAY THREE JOURNAL ENTRY:

DAY FOUR - CHILDREN

Today I am grateful for the lessons little ones teach us. I was reminded of butterfly kisses!

Have you ever heard of butterfly kisses? This is when you bat your eyelashes on another person's cheek. It feels like a butterfly flitting across your cheek. Even thinking about this brings a smile to my face. Share a moment with those whom you care about from your childhood and ask them to share a memory with you.

DAY FOUR JOURNAL ENTRY:

When you begin your day, journal about what you are going to share with those you care for. At the end of the day, enter into your journal what they shared. Was it a childhood memory that brought a smile or was it an adventure they had in their earlier days? As you shared with one another, what happened? Did you find that by sharing stories you learned something new? What a great opportunity to learn more about those we care for.

DAY FOUR JOURNAL ENTRY:

DAY FOUR JOURNAL ENTRY:

DAY FOUR JOURNAL ENTRY:

DAY FIVE -ANGELS

I have many angels here on earth and I am
sending each of you a virtual hug.
I believe that we not only have angels watching over us but we that we have angels here on earth. These individuals may be people you know or they may just show up when you need them. Who are your angels? How have they made a difference in your life?

DAY FIVE JOURNAL ENTRY:

Today, begin your day by reflecting on random acts of kindness that you have had enter your life. Now take a moment and reflect on those random acts of kindnesses that you have bestowed on others. Take time to put these in your journal. As you go through your day today, check back in and record anything new or any memories that have come to you throughout the day.

DAY FIVE JOURNAL ENTRY:

DAY FIVE JOURNAL ENTRY:

DAY FIVE JOURNAL ENTRY:

DAY SIX - SIGNS

We live in such an interesting universe; there are signs everywhere. It is up to us to be open to see, hear and begin to understand them.
What are the signs that are coming up for you today? Maybe it is a song that you hear more than once or something you see repeatedly or even a message on a billboard. Pay attention and see if there is a theme.

DAY SIX JOURNAL ENTRY:

Journal today on what you have noticed as you became aware of any signs and/or themes that came up for you. As you begin to write about the signs you noticed pay attention to the message and contemplate whether there is an underlying message for you. You may even want to talk to others and see if they have ever had such an experience.

DAY SIX JOURNAL ENTRY:

DAY SIX JOURNAL ENTRY:

DAY SIX JOURNAL ENTRY:

DAY SEVEN – QUIET, PEACE

Take the time to enjoy the quiet & peaceful times knowing in your heart that is all that is needed for this moment.

As caregivers, we need to remember to take the time to enjoy the quiet times and peace. We have moments of chaos, yet we survive them. When we experience the moments of peace, we sometimes forget to take the time to relish them. These moments are a gift; don't take them for granted.

DAY SEVEN JOURNAL ENTRY:

For your journal entry today, take time to reflect on the moments when you feel at peace. Make sure to record these moments. What makes them special? Is it the silence or maybe it is something that you associate with music or a sound? Ask someone today what makes them feel at peace and see if this triggers the same response in you.

DAY SEVEN JOURNAL ENTRY:

DAY SEVEN JOURNAL ENTRY:

DAY SEVEN JOURNAL ENTRY:

DAY EIGHT - HICCUPS

Loving life even with occasional "hiccups"!!!! :-)
Wouldn't life be boring if everything went smoothly? The challenge today is to roll with the "hiccups" and see what fabulous things come from them. Instead of holding your breath and trying to get rid of them, breathe allow yourself to just be present in the moment.

DAY EIGHT JOURNAL ENTRY:

Reflect on what it means to be in the moment and how, even when we experience "hiccups," we can remain in the moment. What does this mean for you? Take a few moments and record your thoughts on this.

DAY EIGHT JOURNAL ENTRY:

DAY EIGHT JOURNAL ENTRY:

DAY EIGHT JOURNAL ENTRY:

DAY NINE - LAUGHTER

The biggest thing to remember is that even in the tough times, laughter can lighten the mood.
We get so caught up in "stuff" that sometimes we forget to just laugh. One of the best gifts I have received in caring for my mom, as well as others in my life is to find the humor. Think about when you can find some humor. How it lightens the mood and even has some health benefits, including an endorphin spike!

DAY NINE JOURNAL ENTRY:

Have you heard about laugh yoga? Take a minute and search for it online. Notice how laughter is catchy? Think about something that makes you giggle write about it or better yet, record something you found humorous today.

DAY NINE JOURNAL ENTRY:

DAY NINE JOURNAL ENTRY:

DAY NINE JOURNAL ENTRY:

DAY TEN – REFLECT

Take a moment today and reflect. Are you feeling a little off balance because you are dealing with a lot of things today?

We all have days where, even with the best intentions, things just seem to keep going off track. As caregivers, we all have experienced these days. Look at the situation. Is it critical? Is it something that needs to be dealt with immediately? If not, then let it go for now. You can always reexamine it later and maybe, just maybe, with a fresh outlook the answer appears.

DAY TEN JOURNAL ENTRY:

Take a few minutes and reflect how you can get back on track. What are one or two action steps you can take to lessen the frustration you may be feeling? Record these in your journal and remember that tomorrow is a fresh start.

DAY TEN JOURNAL ENTRY:

DAY TEN JOURNAL ENTRY:

DAY TEN JOURNAL ENTRY:

DAY ELEVEN - ROLLERCOASTER

Here comes the rollercoaster ride, climbing up and up and up and up.......

As caregivers, there are days that feel like you are on a rollercoaster ride climbing up, up, up, up, just waiting to get the top of the ride and then plummeting down and approaching the curve of the ride. Are you able to identify with this? There are times as caregivers we may feel we are doing the same things over and over or may even feel stuck. Remember that routines are not always a bad thing! Consistency may actually be a good thing for your loved one.

DAY ELEVEN JOURNAL ENTRY:

Reflect on your day and take a moment to just breathe. I don't mean one simple breath; I mean a deep breath. Not just one time -- take at least three deep breaths and feel the difference in your body. Now pick up your journal and record your day. Talk about whether you feel you were on a rollercoaster ride or maybe you were on a merry-go-round going around and around. Discuss what your routine is like and whether or not you feel the need to change it. Remember, that as caregivers, we can change our own routines by getting up a few minutes earlier to care for ourselves. Maybe adding a walk into our routine or just sitting outside for a few minutes.

DAY ELEVEN JOURNAL ENTRY:

DAY FIFTEEN JOURNAL ENTRY:

DAY ELEVEN JOURNAL ENTRY:

DAY ELEVEN JOURNAL ENTRY:

DAY TWELVE – POSITIVE THOUGHTS

Ok everybody keep the positive thoughts & prayers coming & I'm sending them back.

Ever had a day like this as a caregiver? Ever felt so overwhelmed you just need some positive thoughts sent your way? As you read this, think about the fact that others before you have felt the same way and are now sending positive thoughts to you.

DAY TWELVE JOURNAL ENTRY:

As you read this message today, you realized you really aren't alone. There are so many people that are caregivers. They may not be able to reach out to you physically but they are there for you. As you think about this, record any thoughts or feelings you may have about this. Remember also that if you feel isolated, you may want to reach out to someone in your community for support.

DAY TWELVE JOURNAL ENTRY:

DAY TWELVE JOURNAL ENTRY:

DAY TWELVE JOURNAL ENTRY:

DAY THIRTEEN – CAPTURE THE MOMENT

Remember to take a moment, breathe and take a snapshot of that moment for your memory album.
As we go through our busy day, we often forget to take a moment, pause and add that memory to our memory album. When we do this, we can have these moments later in life. You may even want to take an actual picture so you have them later. In today's day and time, think how easy it is to take a picture with your phone, then email it to yourself, add it to an album on your computer or print it out.

DAY THIRTEEN JOURNAL ENTRY:

Reflect back over your day and pull out moments from your day. Ask yourself what was special about that moment. Some of the best times we have with our loved ones are just being present. We don't always have to be going somewhere. Take a moment and just hold their hand, feel the energy that passes between the two of you. We don't always need words. Remember, just being present in the moment is all that is needed. Record a moment of just being present in your journal.

DAY THIRTEEN JOURNAL ENTRY:

DAY THIRTEEN JOURNAL ENTRY:

DAY THIRTEEN JOURNAL ENTRY:

DAY FOURTEEN – REFLECT

Love life and live it to the fullest each day. Spend time with the ones you love. And remember to laugh often :-)

As we care for those around us, we, as caregivers, need to remember the importance of taking time to reflect and enjoy the moment. Laughter is a continuous theme in my book as is taking time to reflect. Each day and each moment of that day is a precious gift that has been given to us.

DAY FOURTEEN JOURNAL ENTRY:

Reflecting on your day, what is the one special moment that you want to record? Why is this moment of this day so precious? What happened? What were the sights, sounds and smells etc. that surrounded this moment? Take time to record as much detail as you can. Create a record of this moment.

DAY FOURTEEN JOURNAL ENTRY:

DAY FOURTEEN JOURNAL ENTRY:

DAY FOURTEEN JOURNAL ENTRY:

DAY FIFTEEN - COMPLAINING

Complaining gets us nowhere. For today, if I feel like I want to complain, I am changing that to a compliment and a smile!

It would be so easy for us to just complain. It is more empowering to change that complaint into something positive, like a compliment. Remember that old saying, "you get further with honey than with vinegar"; this applies to our everyday lives and really does work.

DAY FIFTEEN JOURNAL ENTRY:

Take a moment and record in your journal a time today when you changed a complaint into a positive moment. How did you do this? What changed when you did this? Did you find that not only your mood but also those around you changed and lightened up?

DAY FIFTEEN JOURNAL ENTRY:

DAY FIFTEEN JOURNAL ENTRY:

DAY SIXTEEN - LEGACY

I have entitled this as "the Epitaph." What kind of person do I want to be remembered as -- the complacent one or the adventurer?

As a caregiver we sometimes get lost in the identity of those we care for. This quote is to assist you by reminding you that you have your own identity.

DAY SIXTEEN JOURNAL ENTRY:

I am asking you to take a moment to reflect on what you want your legacy to be today. Take time to reflect on how you want to be remembered. What do you want to impart to others? What would you like others to remember about you? Are you the person who enjoys life and lives it to the fullest? Take a moment and record in your journal what it is. This exercise is a gentle reminder that you are more than a caregiver; you are also an individual with a life outside of caring for others. Play with this and challenge yourself to think outside the box!

DAY SIXTEEN JOURNAL ENTRY:

DAY SIXTEEN JOURNAL ENTRY:

DAY SIXTEEN JOURNAL ENTRY:

DAY SEVENTEEN – THANK YOU

Remember to thank someone who has meaning in your life today.

This is a gentle reminder to reach out and thank someone who is special in your life. We get so busy with our day- to- day routines that we are on what I like to call automatic pilot and "assume" that those who are special in our life know it. Today take the time to say and/or demonstrate this in a way that is meaningful.

DAY SEVENTEEN JOURNAL ENTRY:

For today's entry, record who you reached out to and what was their reaction? How did you feel when you let them know what they meant to you? How are you feeling now recording this in your journal? Take a moment and just be present with this feeling. Take those deep breaths I spoke about earlier in this journey. Now how do you feel?

DAY SEVENTEEN JOURNAL ENTRY:

DAY SEVENTEEN JOURNAL ENTRY:

DAY SEVENTEEN JOURNAL ENTRY:

DAY EIGHTEEN - CHALLENGES

Challenges are given to us as a gift. It is up to us to unwrap it and see what lies underneath the packaging.

So many times we look at difficult times as just that – difficult. Today choose to look at the situation in a different light, see it as a challenge. See how that changes your approach and attitude.

DAY EIGHTEEN JOURNAL ENTRY:

Look back over the day and see the challenges that have arisen. Did the experience change when you chose to see it as a challenge? What feeling came up from this experience? Was it easier to look at the situation as a challenge versus a problem or a difficult situation?

DAY EIGHTEEN JOURNAL ENTRY:

DAY EIGHTEEN JOURNAL ENTRY:

DAY EIGHTEEN JOURNAL ENTRY:

DAY NINETEEN – STRENGTH, WISDOM, GRACE

Strength, Wisdom and Grace: Strength to accept, Wisdom to know it will pass and Grace to allow it to happen as it should.

These are powerful words to reflect on throughout the day. We all have and need these components as caregivers. We have strength to accept the moment and strength to assist others in their journey. We have wisdom to know that the moment passes when we feel inadequate or overwhelmed and we acquire grace as we care for individuals.

DAY NINETEEN JOURNAL ENTRY:

At the end of the day, record how you have strength, wisdom and grace and how this allows you to carry on as a caregiver. Why are these important, not just in your role as a caregiver, but also in your other roles, be they mother, father, sister, brother, wife, husband, friend or lover.

DAY NINETEEN JOURNAL ENTRY:

DAY NINETEEN JOURNAL ENTRY:

DAY NINETEEN JOURNAL ENTRY:

DAY TWENTY – LESSONS

Today think about all the people who have entered into and out of your life and the lessons that you took away from the experiences.

This is a great exercise to begin and end your day. Take a moment to examine your life and how you have come so far. Think back about those individuals who have had an influence in your life and have helped you grow into the person you are today.

DAY TWENTY JOURNAL ENTRY:

Enter into your journal those individuals who have provided you with growing moments. Keep in mind that there are those who have had more influence than others. List out what they have contributed to your growth. Want to take it to the next level? Find one person on this list to send a letter of gratitude. Let them know how much they have meant to you. If they are no longer here on earth and they are the number one person who has influenced you, write the letter and tuck it away. How do you feel after you have written to them? If they are here and you know how to locate them, send them the letter. It is a great way to surprise someone who has been special in your life.

DAY TWENTY JOURNAL ENTRY:

DAY TWENTY JOURNAL ENTRY:

DAY TWENTY JOURNAL ENTRY:

DAY TWENTY ONE - HAPPINESS

How many times have we mistaken that happiness comes from an outside source? Actually happiness emanates from inside of us and affects those around us.

Look at this statement more than once. Think about a time when you were really happy and how that influenced the people around you. Think about a time you came across someone who was just bubbling with happiness. Wasn't it catchy? It's hard to remain grumpy around someone when they are happy. Play with this today and see what changes around you.

DAY TWENTY-ONE JOURNAL ENTRY:

Your entry at the end of the day is to write about how you influenced others around you with your happiness. What were their reactions? How do you feel at the end of this day?

DAY TWENTY-ONE JOURNAL ENTRY:

DAY TWENTY-ONE JOURNAL ENTRY:

DAY TWENTY-ONE JOURNAL ENTRY:

DAY TWENTY TWO - BLESSINGS

I look at each day as a precious memory. Each moment of each day is such a blessing.

Earlier in this journey I asked you to record special moments in your memory album. Today I want you to reflect on your blessings this day has provided for you.

DAY TWENTY-TWO JOURNAL ENTRY:

This journal entry is to be done at the beginning and the end of the day. At the beginning of the day reflect on your past, record up to five blessings that have entered into your life. At the end of the day record at least one blessing that has entered into your life.

DAY TWENTY-TWO JOURNAL ENTRY:

DAY TWENTY-TWO JOURNAL ENTRY:

DAY TWENTY-TWO JOURNAL ENTRY:

DAY TWENTY THREE - MOMENTS

Remember to breathe! :-) If we all took a moment out of each and every day to just sit in silence and take in a deep breath and smile. I wonder..........

What would happen if we took a moment of silence and just took a breath before we launched into the day? How would this affect our demeanor? So often we just wake up and start our daily routine. There are different ways we could incorporate this into our routine. While we are taking our shower we could take some deep breaths, while we are getting dressed for our day we could set aside a few minutes to just breathe. Meditation has been proven to help in so many ways lowering blood pressure, adding energy, take some baby steps and practice breathing.

DAY TWENTY-THREE JOURNAL ENTRY:

Today take a moment and record how you feel as you begin your day. Take pauses throughout the day to breathe. At the end of the day record if your day was different because you took little "moments" throughout your day.

DAY TWENTY-THREE JOURNAL ENTRY:

DAY TWENTY-THREE JOURNAL ENTRY:

DAY TWENTY-THREE JOURNAL ENTRY:

DAY TWENTY FOUR – GRATITUDE ATTITUDE

Start this day with a new attitude and plenty of gratitude.

We have all heard about gratitude and how incorporating it into our daily lives is beneficial. If you haven't heard this news bulletin, you have now! Today, take a moment to think about the things you are grateful for, as the day progresses make a mental note of those things.

DAY TWENTY-FOUR JOURNAL ENTRY:

Record at the beginning of the day five things you are grateful for. They don't have to be material things; they can be moments, people or things. Still motivated? Take a few minutes at the end of the day and record one or two.

DAY TWENTY-FOUR JOURNAL ENTRY:

DAY TWENTY-FOUR JOURNAL ENTRY:

DAY TWENTY-FOUR JOURNAL ENTRY:

DAY TWENTY FIVE - SURPRISES

Grateful for unexpected surprises!!! :-)
Unexpected surprises are wonderful. Have you had any recently? Think about what they are and how they affected you. Think about a time you have given someone an unexpected surprise. One thing to remember today is that surprises don't have to be large or expensive to make an impact. A lot of times it is the small things that are appreciated the most. Offering to do one nice thing for someone else can be the biggest and best surprise! It may not seem like much to you, but it could be the blessing they need. Want an example? Why not make a dinner and take it to someone? Offer to take someone to the doctor or just take to time to call to see how they are doing.

DAY TWENTY-FIVE JOURNAL ENTRY:

Enter into your journal a time when you provided someone with an unexpected surprise. How did you feel? How did the other person react? What about an unexpected surprise that came your way, how did you feel? Who or what was the surprise?

DAY TWENTY-FIVE JOURNAL ENTRY:

DAY TWENTY-FIVE JOURNAL ENTRY:

DAY TWENTY-FIVE JOURNAL ENTRY:

DAY TWENTY SIX - CELEBRATE

Happiness is in each of us. Sometimes we just have to dig a little deeper to find it.

As caregivers, we get overwhelmed and forget to celebrate the little moments. So today, take the time to celebrate those moments. Maybe buy yourself some flowers or treat yourself to a spa day. It is not selfish to take some time for yourself. It is imperative you make the time to take care of yourself so you can then in turn care for those around you. It can be as simple as taking five minutes out of your busy day and writing in your journal or picking up a magazine and reading an article that you have wanted to catch up on. It could even be taking a walk, even a short one, around the block. Just take the time to celebrate you!

DAY TWENTY-SIX JOURNAL ENTRY:

What was the moment you chose to celebrate? Why? Did you take the time to share what you were celebrating with anyone else? Who and why? How did you share this moment?

DAY TWENTY-SIX JOURNAL ENTRY:

DAY TWENTY-SIX JOURNAL ENTRY:

DAY TWENTY-SIX JOURNAL ENTRY:

DAY TWENTY SEVEN - A NEW DAY

I love the fact that each day is a new beginning.
The greatest gift we can give ourselves is permission to begin each day as a new one. We chose to not carry over the "stuff" from the day before. Today is fresh. When we start our days like this, it lightens the load.

DAY TWENTY-SEVEN JOURNAL ENTRY

Begin your day with journaling about how you want your day to go. As the day progresses, reflect back on your journal entry. Watch how your day unfolds. We can choose to have a day that is filled with light and love. Remember to share this with someone.

DAY TWENTY-SEVEN JOURNAL ENTRY:

DAY TWENTY-SEVEN JOURNAL ENTRY:

DAY TWENTY-SEVEN JOURNAL ENTRY:

DAY TWENTY EIGHT - TRUST

Trust and control do not go together.

Let's examine this statement. What does it mean for you? As a caregiver, I have learned that I don't need nor want to control a situation. I would much rather develop trust rather than to try control the person or situation. I have also learned that the illusion of control may help get us through the moment but in the long run I have always reflected back and wondered, "What was I trying to accomplish?" "Did I succeed by trying to force the situation?" Most of the time the answer is "I don't know" and "definitely not" in succeeding.

DAY TWENTY-EIGHT JOURNAL ENTRY:

What does control mean to you? What does trust look and feel like for you? What does it mean for you to have trust with someone? Remember, that if we try to control a situation, then it may not go the way we want it to. Take a step back and take a breath and ask what is more important, control or trust? Write about this.

DAY TWENTY-EIGHT JOURNAL ENTRY:

DAY TWENTY-EIGHT JOURNAL ENTRY:

DAY TWENTY-EIGHT JOURNAL ENTRY:

DAY TWENTY NINE - CHARACTER

Each day has a beginning and an ending. What we do in between determines our character.

As caregivers, we can get so caught up in the moment we forget that what we do, say and act like reflects back on us. If we could take a moment and think before we react to a situation, we may not have to do any back pedaling.

DAY TWENTY-NINE JOURNAL ENTRY:

At the end of the day, record a moment that you took a "pause for the cause." How did you feel? Was this situation lightened because you took a moment? What happened? How did those individuals around you react?

DAY TWENTY-NINE JOURNAL ENTRY:

DAY TWENTY-NINE JOURNAL ENTRY:

DAY TWENTY-NINE JOURNAL ENTRY:

DAY THIRTY - POSITIVE

When we change our self-limiting thoughts to positive, uplifting thoughts, it not only changes how we feel but it changes how we interact with others.

Changing our thought process and increasing our positivity does not mean we are "Pollyannas." What it does mean is that we look for the good in situations, people and places. When you begin the journey of looking for the positive, you may also notice how often you have complained or looked at something in a negative manner. I just want you to know that is okay. It is part of learning and growing. It is actually a good thing because now you are noticing and can change the behavior if you want to. So don't become overly critical of yourself; just look at it as part of the learning curve!

DAY THIRTY JOURNAL ENTRY:

How are you positive? How have you grown and changed in the last month by taking time for yourself either at the beginning or ending of the day. What has changed about you and what have you chosen to keep the same?

DAY THIRTY JOURNAL ENTRY:

DAY THIRTY JOURNAL ENTRY:

DAY THIRTY JOURNAL ENTRY:

DAY THIRTY ONE - EMBRACE

I embrace the past me because it led to where I am presently. I celebrate the future me and look forward to the journey.

My wish for everyone who has taken the time to read and journal each day this past month is that you see how much you have grown. I hope you take away with you the gifts of not only caring for others but the importance of caring for yourself.

DAY THIRTY-ONE JOURNAL ENTRY:

When you look at yourself, have you increased your vocabulary with words that are more empowering? Have others commented to you that they see a change in you? Has your interactions with others improved? If you answered in the affirmative to any of these questions, I want you to give yourself an angel's hug! Wrap your arms around yourself and squeeze tightly!

DAY THIRTY-ONE JOURNAL ENTRY:

DAY THIRTY-ONE JOURNAL ENTRY:

DAY THIRTY-ONE JOURNAL ENTRY:

CONCLUSION

I hope you have enjoyed the past month's journey. If you like the book help spread the word about it. Pass it along, talk about it, encourage others to read it. Help the cause of caring for the caregiver. Join my Facebook page "Daily Inspirations for Caregivers." I am so excited to see the ideas and thoughts of those who have read this book. Please take a moment to record them on the Facebook page or feel free to contact me through my website:

www.theuathenticitycoach.com

ABOUT THE AUTHOR

JUDY MICALE

Judy Micale is a Business, Life & Wellness Coach. In this capacity she encourages clients to grow both professionally and personally. Working with individuals and organizations as a coach and consultant, Judy provides a variety of services with training and workshops that embrace strategic gratitude, a balanced life, compassion fatigue and a focus on the strengths that a person already has.

"Focus on your strengths and watch the ripple effect around you." That is the banner on Judy's website, www.theauthenticitycoach.com

Judy claims the greatest pleasure she receives from her work is the love of "assisting others in their journey, whether it is helping them stay accountable to their goals and actions or exploring what it is they want to do next in their life or business."

Judy offers mini retreats, group coaching and other opportunities to share her extensive talents, including lunch & learn style programs. Also, add in keynote presentations and other speaking engagements.

Judy lives in Tallahassee with her "84 years young" Mom and two pups: Laci, a 13-year-old poodle and Chelsea, a 2-year-old Maltipoo. Her music preference is everything from R&B, Big Band, Opera, New Age.......... definitely a diverse taste.

Judy's Bliss: "My bliss comes from living each day with gratitude, walking the walk I talk. "

Words of wisdom: "Each day is a gift that we have received. If we live each day with this thought in the back of our minds then the possibilities are endless."

Want to contact Judy or learn a little bit more about her as a coach and motivational speaker? Go to her website www.theauthenticitycoach.com